Fool to have thrown it all away

Confessions of a narc survivor
Poems and reflection pages

Meenakshi Sukumaran

BookLeaf Publishing
India | USA | UK

Made with ❤ on the BookLeaf Publishing Platform
www.bookleafpub.in
www.bookleafpub.com

To all those who have loved a narc and lost,
obviously

You are not alone.

To him, for supplying me with all the material to write about.

This wouldn't have been possible without you.

Meenakshi Sukumaran is not my real name.
Everything else said in this book is true.

Preface

WARNING: Some of the poems in this book can be triggering if you are or have been abused by a narcissist.

The purpose of this book was firstly to give an outlet to my own abusive experience with a narcissistic husband. As the poems flowed onto the pages, a new awareness emerged. I realized their power in helping people in such relationships to become aware that what they are experiencing is abuse in the first place. It took me more than a decade to get clarity and courage. It takes time.

Journaling has always been my refuge for untangling the web of thoughts in my head and transitioning from thoughts to feelings to action.

If you are a narc survivor, you can use this book as a guided journal. I have added prompts after each poem that would assist you in understanding your situation.

While my experience has been with my husband, narcissism is not relationship- or gender-specific.

If you don't feel like writing to the prompts at the moment, keep the question in mind as you go for a walk, take a shower, or do anything that helps you to bring awareness of your experiences to the forefront, and try to unpack them. Awareness is the first step on the road to healing.

Join me on this journey of healing.

The quietest girl

The quietest girl

Who was I?
The quietest girl growing up
Doted for my invisibility
A shitty marriage
A choice to be dominated
Made by conditioning
Years of unlearning
Reclaiming my soul

The inner voice
Muffled for long
Incoherent, mumbling
Until realization dawned
That unconditional self-love is
Homecoming at last

Break this cycle
Raise your daughters
To trust their instincts
Holding firm boundaries
Strong, wild, and free.

Notes to self

What choices do I seem to be conditioned to make repeatedly?

How I reclaimed my soul

I learnt child psychology through an intensive teacher training program. I understood that my lack of trust in my instincts and my own choices, neediness, and lack of self-worth stemmed from authoritative parenting. Once I realized that, I could love my inner child and start my healing journey.

Growing spiritually helped. The Power of Now by Eckhart Tolle was transformative for me. Sadhguru's talks and inner engineering online gave me strength.

I picked books* that resonated with my needs at that moment and listened to them on Audible while doing chores. Every book had at least one life-altering insight that I became conscious of and slowly began imbibing them.

**I have listed the books and YouTube channels that I found useful at the end of this book.*

Notes to self

Three things that I am willing to begin doing, that will show me the way to healing:

“Some changes look negative on the surface but you will soon realise that space is being created in your life for something new to emerge.”

Eckhart Tolle

Hot and cold

Hot and cold

Hot and cold
Like a see-saw
Hot was hope
Burning bright a few days
Winters were long, chilly
Icy and grey
Cycle went on
Days became years in a haze
Before my soul eroded and erupted
Unsnarling the knots
Off the depths of narcissism
And realized
This too was abuse.

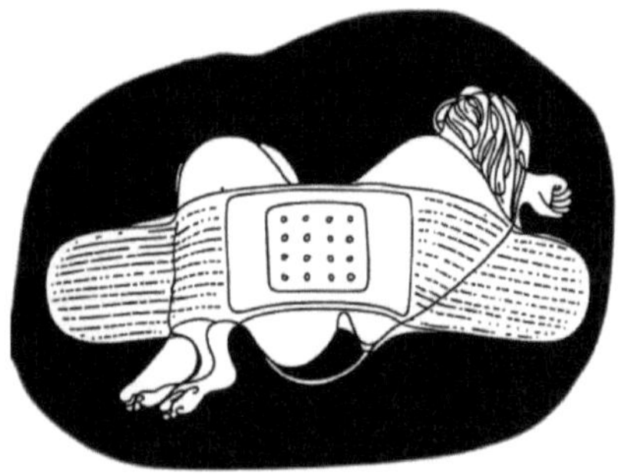

Notes to self

What repetitive patterns do I see in my relationship that seem to be sucking my energy out?

How I recognized the pattern of hot and cold

Narcissists pick a person who is vulnerable, needy, has low self-esteem, and has a giving heart. Such a person will give the benefit of the doubt to their abuser for a long time, making excuses on their behalf, before they are roughly jolted into awareness.

I saw that whenever he needed something from me, like an upcoming visit to his family, he put on an act of being the perfect husband. The day we returned home, he was a different, very nasty person. This happened over and over and over again.

We were happy for two to three days when he would love-bomb me. Then he would pick a fight for something trivial. The fight went on for a week or a fortnight until he needed physical intimacy. He used physical intimacy also as a means to confuse me about his undying love.

These extremes were exceedingly painful because every good phase brought hope, only to be shattered. As I started voicing these patterns to him and my friends, it began to dawn on me. My inner voice said this is not how it is supposed to be and that this person does not want to live happily.

Notes to self

Three people who are strong role models for me and with whom I will discuss the patterns that I am observing:

"The fear of loss is the driver of emotional behaviour for every human being on the planet."

Chris Voss

Sniggering

Sniggering

They deserve this treatment,
These lowly creatures.
Their mere presence,
A blight on my existence.
From my lofty perch,
I see their pettiness,
A laughable, pathetic farce.
Servants, all of them,
Existing to fulfil my desires.
Waiters, maids, drivers,
Delivery boys, call center liars.
Every penny, every moment,
Owed to me,
A divine right,
Eternally.
So he thinks.

Notes to self

Narcs detest people of a lower status or those of no use to them. Let me note down instances of sniggering that I have observed:

How I responded to such behavior

Initially, I found this behavior very triggering. I would burst out in indignation as to how he could be so disrespectful to people who provided services to us.

I decided to give consequences. I stopped looking for maids when they quit because of his lack of manners. The kitchen sink would be filled with utensils, and I would not touch it. He automatically curbed his behavior.

When it was not in my control, for example, when he dragged on with the credit card rep for hours to waive paltry late payment fees, I simply moved out of hearing range and busied myself elsewhere.

Meditation helped put a distance between his behavior and my emotions. I could look at him as if he was a drunk man on the road causing a ruckus and who did not matter to me.

Notes to self

Does their behavior with others trigger me? In what ways? What consequence will I give them and how will I detach?

"A narcissist without narcissistic supply is as empty and as manically depressed, panicked, nasty or catatonic as any hardcore drug addict unable to score."

Melanie Tonia Evans

Odd hours

Odd hours

3 AM
a nudge, a tug,
a whispered demand in the dark.
Groggy, weary,
a life of endless tasks.
Office, kitchen, kids,
a constant, relentless routine
Sleep, a distant dream
The alarm's harsh cry,
a 6 AM sigh
"Let me sleep," I plead,
a tired, desperate need.
"But I want it," he demands,
a selfish, heartless command.
Years of surrender,
a life of despair.
Stolen sleep,
an endless, nightmarish affair.
Unearthly hours,
a constant, cruel test.
Fights picked,
right before bedtime
Naps interrupted

with doors banged
Sleep-deprived,
a zombie, at best.
Leaving for work,
a hollow, weary frame,

Unaware of the damage.
The sleep-deprived game.

How I recognized sleep deprivation as a form of abuse

I did not, for almost a decade! It happened every night. Even when he did not initiate sex, he would wake me up and go back to sleep snoring. Pure evil.

Sometimes I slept off in my children's bed while making them sleep. In the morning, I would feel very fresh, even though there was barely any room for me. That's when I realized I was missing out on proper sleep.

While reading about narcissism a few years ago, I came across a post on the sleep-deprivation tactics of narcissists. My jaw dropped when I realized that I had been a victim all along! He stopped after I complained to the police. Now I sleep in another room with the door locked.

Notes to self

Does this person consistently do things to ensure that I do not get rest when I need it?

"You become very very powerful when you overcome yourself."

David Goggins

Personal space

Personal space

Funny, loud, brash
He's like that only
Roasts without a care
A callous display
Men laugh and bond, asking for more
Gesturing and waving
Flailing arms far and wide
Invading personal space
Many close calls, near misses
A disregard for boundaries,
But oh, the right words, in polite company,
A mask of charm, a facade for all to see.
"Heart's in the right place," they say,
Charader in plain view.

Notes to self

How does this person create a favorable impression in front of others? How do they manage a superior stature outside the home?

How I am trying to protect my circle from being influenced by him

I have told my story to my circle of people. They don't need any convincing. They have also caught the sly vibrations behind his facade, even though they have been unsure of their initial perceptions. Sharing my story was necessary so that they were not hoodwinked.

I skip social gatherings where I feel like an intruder in his circle. I may come across as 'cold' to his people because I don't reciprocate his overtures. It may result in being labelled asocial, but I choose my peace of mind.

I am growing my tribe by finding people who match my wavelength.

Notes to self

How will I grow my tribe?

"It's their way of reminding who is in control, and it works. Even when they are not physically close, they will dominate the conversation by talking over you."

Danish Bashir

No time for me

No time for me

Balcony garden, I thought
Sat working with newly bought plants
“This is what you have time for?
With a small child at home?”
My heart shrivelled
Gardening didn't appeal anymore

Books were my haven
Sat reading next to him
“You don't have time for me
Is this necessary?”
Putting the book down, I said
“Ok, let's talk”
His eyes never left the screen
A silent contempt
Heart-to-heart conversation
Wasn’this thing
Reading died too.

Notes to self

What things that I loved doing has this person taken the joy out of? How do they do it?

What I wish I had done when he stopped me from doing things I loved

Narcs are very weak people inside. They crumble when your defences are strong.

If I had been steely, which I was not, and which is why he chose me, he would have backed off. I realized this once I stopped heeding his negative commentary and snubs.

This doesn't mean he would not try to sabotage things behind my back or not run a smear campaign to misinform people about my character. That's another battle.

Notes to self

Let me list down 3 worthwhile things that I want to do right now. What will be my first step toward actioning each of them?

“A narcissist doesn’t break your heart. They break your spirit. That’s why it takes so long to heal.”

Anonymous

Shopping blues

Shopping blues

First few years
Took him shopping for me
He, the stylist
Selecting clothes with a
Confident flourish
"I've better taste," he'd boast
A patronizing tone

Now I'm no model figure
Fantasize how much ever he may!
Emerging from the trial room
His sniggering gaze
Critical and assessing
A rude snap on a tight sleeve
An impatient pull at a catch in the waist
Digging my toes into the floor
Tears welling, I'd resign
"Let's come another time."

In time, put a full-stop
Found my voice
My own style
Learned my body, its curves, its grace

Developed a taste

Wish I had all of it before
Would have saved me
A lifetime of self-doubt
The burden of self-imposed exile
The sting of love unrequited
And the ache of an ill-fitting relationship

How I developed a positive body image

Developing a positive self-image has taken years of healing—meditation, listening to talks by experts in the field of narc abuse, undergoing healing sessions including inner-child healing, journaling, giving priority to self-care, and not to mention developing a fashion sense as per my body type.

I had to learn that it was okay to spend money on myself while being judicious about it. I buy for an occasion and don't hoard unnecessarily. That way I have the right clothes to wear that I cherish.

I began receiving compliments saying I have great taste now and that my personality radiated a glow. I felt I had emerged from his vile shadow into my soulful light.

Notes to self

How does this person make me doubt my self-image—physical, behavioral, emotional, spiritual—any facet of my personality?

"Beauty begins the moment you decide to be yourself."

Coco Chanel

Smear campaign

Smear campaign

They never tell the full story,
Only the fragments that paint you pale

Guests brought in unannounced,
A living room laid bare,
A chaotic, messy tableau.

"She orders food on weekends,"
A judgmental refrain,
Ignoring the weekday grind,
The 6 AM starts, and the 11 PM wraps.
While my lord,
A master of the art of leisure,
Indulges in perpetual bed-rest,
Twiddling his thumbs.

Couple selfies taken in a split-second
Sneaked-in against will
In a playful moment with kids
I relented to preserve the mood
It made a perfect couple image
For his 'cute' DP
Or does it?

He's trying at least, so it seems

Instances like these trivial
Make a flimsy story
Who would believe?
Agony behind closed doors
Unseen, underestimated
They never show you the full
picture...
Only the parts where they look
charming.

How I coped with smear campaigns

It's not possible to be constantly looking out to correct my image whenever he tries to tarnish it. Narcs are relentless. They derive energy from debasing others. Trying to undo their smear will only wear you out.

All I can do is live a wholesome life. Living in a cave will not help, for sure. People need to see me for the person I am and the person I am not. Maintaining contact with people around me and sharing my story is important.

Living with this narc has made me super-efficient and super-smart as I tried to preempt every criticism and become good at every possible thing. What started as a fear response became a personal goal to live life to the fullest. I am proud of the person I have become. I live in peace because I am not competing with him for one-upmanship, and I feel sorry that he can only keep looking for things to disgrace me.

Notes to self

What are the three areas that I feel I should improve myself in (irrespective of the narc's criticism)?

“Peace is found when we become okay with being misunderstood by others.”

Unknown

PhD

PhD

A know-it-all doesn't know
That he doesn't know it all
That paraphrasing in preachy words
Is a giveaway
Takes years of toil
A hundred streams of knowledge
Each a universe to explore
Demanding respect
And a thirst to dig deeper
If he knew it all,
The Creator himself, perhaps he would be
Pointless to retort
Shunning futile debates
I decided, let God be God.

Notes to self

What examples of know-it-all behaviour have I witnessed in the narc in my life?

How I get through this know-it-all behavior

Initially, I used to cringe at his PhD behavior, because while they try to project a lofty image, narcs are bound to be 'found out'. I used to blurt out corrections, which he would then rephrase as HIS thought! Pointless.

With time, I calmed myself down and became an amused observer who would not even raise an eyebrow to jaw-dropping theories. I just saw him as a drunk man on the street who did not deserve my attention.

People who spend enough time with him and are also sensible will realize this eventually.

Notes to self

What thoughts course through my mind, and how does my body react when this person behaves like a know-it-all? How will I calm myself next time?

"You have power over your mind – not outside events. Realize this, and you will find strength."

Marcus Aurelius

East-west

East-west

"Chinese, huh?"
    "Pizza sounds good to me."
"Bright lights?"
    "Dim, definitely."
"Home remedy?"
    "Medicine, of course, it's the best medicine."
"This outfit?"
    "Does that one not fit anymore?"

A strange feeling, a nagging doubt,
Did he default west when I say east?
Decided to test

"Dinner tonight, cooking a special!"
    "Why bother, eating out will be fun!"

Works for me! ;)
A winning smile fading

Such a play
Tiresome to sustain
Shrewd alertness

Plotting every move
Walking on eggshells
Crafty love
Not my cup of tea
Truth being —
This wasn't about choices
This was about control

How I handled this controlling behavior

The first step was to notice that it was happening consistently. For anything that brought a spark of joy in my eyes—he sabotaged it deliberately.

Secondly, I paused before candidly sharing my wish or plan. Sometimes I played the reverse game—saying the opposite of what I wanted. At other times, I moved myself out of the equation. When he made plans for something he knew I would not enjoy or like, I declined to participate.

Whether or not he chose to contradict me, I had already made my decision and stated it firmly. I would not sway from it.

Thirdly, I detached and created a parallel life in which he had no part to play. We practically live as roommates in the same house today. I will divorce him when it is least disruptive for my children.

For a person who has been controlled for long, remember it is a journey coming out of it and not a one-step solution.

Please note—this is my choice of actions. What you choose to do will be guided by your unique circumstances.

Notes to self

How is this person manipulating my choices? What will I do differently and smartly from now on so that my choices are secure?

“The narcissist consumes people, devours their output and casts their empty, writhing shells aside.”

Dr. Sam Vaknin

Fool to have thrown it all away

Fool to have thrown it all away

Blessed with a wife who loved his family
Children raised well
Healthful eating habits
Double-income household,
affording a good life
A lovely home
Couldn't keep it together
Money, control; a selfish, twisted core
a fool's curse forever
And yet I mourn
not for him
but for life poured
into a bottomless well

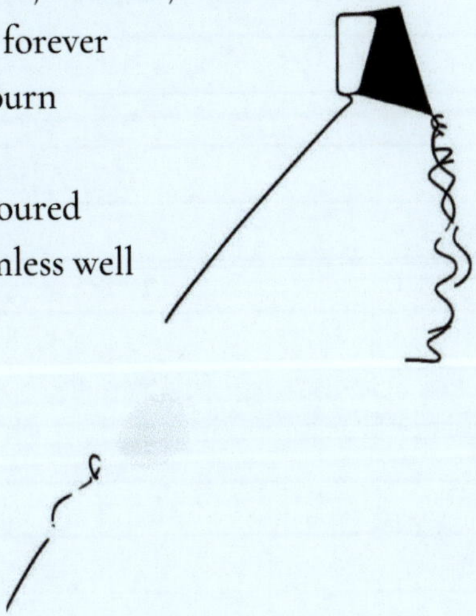

Notes to self

How have I poured into a bottomless well in this relationship?

What I feel today about a lifetime spent with this person

If I could go back and make a different choice, I would not marry this person. Absolutely not. No one in their sane mind would.

But I also believe in the laws of karma. He was meant to come into my life to teach me some lessons. The hardships molded me into a stronger,better person, and I am thankful to him for that.

Our journey ends here and I have mentally released him peacefully, effortlessly, and agreeably.

I will live the rest of my life in ways that serve my soul and not by suppressing my needs and emotions.

Notes to self

When I reflect on my life with this person, what has this experience taught me? How do I live serving my soul in the highest possible way?

"How deeply you touch another life is how rich your life is."

Sadhguru

I'm sorry, but...

I'm sorry, but...

I'm sorry I shouted
But... you should've remembered
Sorry, I said nasty things,
But... I like my food just right
Sorry for cursing and swearing
But... you test my patience

Don't be fooled, oh blind lover—
The sorry, a mask, a flimsy disguise
With a "but" that lingers, a cruel surprise
A sorry that ends with a but
Is responsibility shunned
A guilt undone

Notes to self

Have I observed fake apologies from this person? What forms of sugar-coating do they resort to, to mask their wrongdoings?

How I respond to the "sorry-buts" today

I don't care to listen to them.

When he comes with an apology, inevitably followed by an explanation of how I was the reason for his behavior, I simply smile or shrug or laugh it off, saying—"Of course, it's my mistake" or "I am the most useless person in the world. I know that by now. Be happy; it's not your fault."

At other times, I simply tell him in very few words that I don't have time for an explanation and that it doesn't matter what he thinks of me.

Since he doesn't get any narcissistic supply from me now, he has stopped bothering me. It is no longer worth his time because he can't make me feel bad about myself.

Notes to self

What short, sensible responses can I frame to shut the narc up when they come up with a fake apology?

"Narcissists don't have relationships. They have hostages."

Dr. Ramani Durvasula

I never stopped you

I never stopped you

Stop blaming me for not celebrating
A single festival with your family
I never hindered your familial ties
We were just short of leaves

Stop being dramatic
About struggling alone to raise the babies
I never stopped you from getting help
My work kept me preoccupied

Stop complaining
About heart-to-heart conversations,
You could've tried harder,
Men in our family, born reclusive

So I stopped
Giving a damn
About him.

Notes to self

For all the unfairness the narc has meted out to me, how do they turn the story around?

How I stay unaffected by unfair behaviors

Once I healed myself from the trauma, which is also a continuous process of resetting from new ones, I became detached from his deeds. I knew what was to be expected. Once I accepted the fact that a narc can be nothing but evil, and expecting anything else is like wanting the sun to rise from the west, I started living assuming he was not there in my life anymore.

I accepted that if I wanted something to happen, I had to take responsibility for it. If he came in the way, I had to stand my ground and say this is how it will be, and he can choose not to participate.

Thus far, I had built my life around him. I looked for my tribe and found joy with them. If there was no one to share with, I enjoyed my company. When I looked in the mirror, I found someone who would always love me back.

Notes to self

How will I start taking responsibility for my happiness?

"All growth requires loss. A loss of your old values, your old behaviors, your old loves, your old identity. Therefore, growth sometimes has a component of grief to it."

Mark Manson

Curious cat

Curious cat

Watchful eyes
A keen observer
A silent stalker
Eyes scanning the room
Ears attuned to every sound

Peculiar habit—
washing hands in the kitchen sink
A meaningless ritual
Keeping a tab on what's cooking

Spied through the mirror
Like a voyeur
Any unfamiliar rustling
Lazy bum dashed out
Intrigued by my every move
A constant surveillance

So much effort for what?
When he couldn't feel
A heart beating for him

Notes to self

How does the narc in my life keep track of my activities?

How I stop myself from being triggered by constant surveillance

Acceptance of this behavior being the first step, I have taken measures to safeguard my privacy at home. I keep important things under lock and key, carrying the keys with me always.

It requires alertness and can be exhausting at the outset, but as long as we are under the same roof, there is no way around it.

I attend phone calls out of his earshot. When I know he is around, snooping at what I am doing, I just casually look up at him to let him know that I know.

Narcs are quite thick-skinned, so they will do this on purpose to irk you. I play music while doing my chores so that I am not bothered by his presence. It also conveys the message that he is a nobody to me.

Notes to self

What steps will I take to safeguard my privacy?

“I will not bare my soul to their shallow, prying eyes.”

Oscar Wilde

Hidden agenda

Hidden agenda

Trust me
I know your words glazed with sly intentions
Instinct flags caution
As it catches deceitful vibrations
Leech, a parasite, a selfish taker
Pious acts, a mask to impress
Good deeds planned for future payoffs
Timed gifts like artificial sweeteners
Baits on a hook
Emotional bribes
Schemes, calculations, manipulations
Oh, all this while I waited for the most
Precious gift
Of honesty.

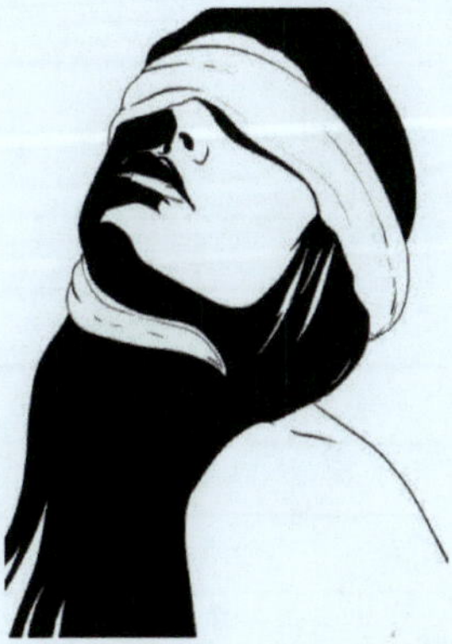

Notes to self

What are some 'good-behavior' instances that I have experienced that turned out to be a hidden agenda of the narc?

How identifying this pattern of good behavior helped me

Once I understood that there was no good behavior without a hidden agenda, I could think a few steps ahead based on the context of the situation to figure out what the narc wanted from me.

I put a full stop to this manipulative behavior by refusing to oblige him for his premeditated good behavior.

Once he knew that I had figured him out and he could no longer extract his wishes from me, he lost interest in putting in effort.

Now the focus has become punitive measures to make me suffer, such as holding back things that he can. But, that is fine with me because 'that' at least has a touch of honesty.

Notes to self

How will I put a full stop to the manipulative behavior of the narc in my life?

“Kicking your own ass only takes one foot off the ground. The same amount of effort could be put into moving forward.”

Chris Voss

Long conversations

Long conversations

Remember staying up
Till the stars faded away
listening to you
Proclaiming your love for me
Though I didn't do enough to deserve

You fought to marry me
Only to be let down
Calling mom daily
And not prioritizing my family, new

Handling finances had to be your domain
Mis-managed as I was
Pocket money from my own salary
A smokescreen of advice
To encroach and occupy
Phew! Good sense prevailed
Didn't take the bait

Conversations with a childhood friend,
Mindless garbage
And improper, you said
Lesbians perhaps?
By some twisted logic

Night after night
Lectures drawled
As I was slowly groomed
To abandon me.

Notes to self

How has the narc tried to groom me to abandon myself and isolate me from the people who love me?

How I recognized the pattern of grooming and isolation

The narc manipulated me to stop talking to my close friends when I was under his control. I spoke to them after seventeen years! - after I regained my sense of self.

Initially, I was about to give him control of my finances, but I got some good counsel in time and decided to keep our finances separate. He could not make me abandon my childhood friend because our bonds were too strong.

Throughout the whole time he was grooming me, my mind questioned his arguments because they did not feel right. But I was like the chained baby elephant, who became an adult and held on to the belief that there was no way to break free from the shackles.

Notes to self

How will I reclaim all that is close to my heart, that I have given up because of the narc?

"I will not stay, not ever again, in a room or conversation, or relationship or institution that requires me to abandon myself."

Glennon Doyle

Flying monkeys

Flying monkeys

He's got his little minions,
His flying monkeys,
Spying, snooping, doing his dirty work.
They report back,
Loyal soldiers,
Believing his every word.

He plants the seeds of doubt,
Waters them with lies,
And watches them grow into a toxic tree.

They buy into his act,
The victim, the innocent one.
Blindly following,
Brainwashed and clueless.
Spoon-fed lies,
They swallow hook, line, and sinker.
Butting their heads into what's
None of their business

To break from his spell,
Defy him once.

Notes to self

Let me make a list of the narc's flying monkeys and what each one does at his behest:

How I deal with the flying monkeys

The first step is to identify that there are flying monkeys.

I don't entertain their inquisitiveness. If they call to sneakily inquire about what I am up to, I give vague answers, and with my tone of voice and responses, I casually make it known that I know this is not a friendly chit-chat.

Being assertive and showing them your boundaries is the only way to deal with flying monkeys.

I am comfortable with being misunderstood because I have come to understand that my worth is not determined by validation from others.

Notes to self

What will I do or say the next time a flying monkey steps into my space?

"This life is mine alone. So I stopped asking people for directions to places they have never been."

Glennon Doyle

Tantrums

Tantrums

A bigger tantrum?
Yeah, good luck finding one
A narcissist scorned
denied control
told a NO
Shown the mirror
proven wrong
ignored
Treated lesser
Left empty-handed
a spoilt child in an adult body
Incorrigible.

Notes to self

Let me list some instances of the narc's temper tantrums that I have faced

How I deal with the narc's temper tantrums

Initially, my response to his tantrums was to give in so that there could be peace. This was like a parent giving in to a spoilt child's never-ending demands.

My fear was the only thing that flared his tantrums. As soon as I became assertive and fearless, he transmuted from a raging bull to a slimy mouse.

When anger didn't work, for some time the preaching sessions followed. But, I firmly refused to give it my time.

Notes to self

What will be some of my response options the next time a tantrum is expected from the narc?

"Daring to set boundaries is about having the courage to love ourselves even when we risk disappointing others."

Brene Brown

Gaslighting

Gaslighting

“That didn't happen,"
a gaslighting game,
questioning reality,
driving me insane.

"You're so careless,"
a hurtful dart,
filling me with shame,
tearing me apart.

"Just a joke,"
a masked sneer,
a sheepish grin,
hiding my fear.

"No big deal,"
a dismissive decree,
a battle within,
a lost identity.

"I didn't say that,"
a twisted lie,

a mind confused,
a questioning cry.

"Don't get upset,"
a patronizing tone,
a constant state of unease,
a soul overthrown.

A house of cards,
a fragile, fleeting sight,
reality slipping away,
a fading light.

Am I losing my mind,
or is this a cruel design?

Notes to self

Let me list down some instances of gaslighting when the narc has made me question my reality:

How I deal with gaslighting

Narcs retreat when confronted with facts. When I started stating plain facts to his baseless arguments, he knew I could not be played anymore. Of course, he would refute those as well when possible, but inside he knew that it was 'game over'.

My responses after that became very monotonous and brief, such as—Please leave; This discussion is pointless; I am not interested in this conversation—which I would repeat like a stuck record. Narcs cannot take the sheer boringness of this response when they can't get anything out of you.

I would smirk and have a barely-there, amused smile when he tried gaslighting. It irked him to no end.

Notes to self

What are some brief, standard responses that I can have when the narc gaslights me?

“The closer you are in alignment with what you want, the calmer it feels.”

Abraham Hicks

Expletives

Expletives

A universe revolves around them,
A black hole sucking all the light.
Always ready to claim the throne,
Never lifting a finger, a parasite.
A spotlight hogger,
A taker, not a giver.
A master manipulator,
A deceitful, conniving liver.
A boundary-smasher,
A promise-breaker,
A heart as cold as winter's weather.
A soul devoid of empathy,
A toxic nightmare, eternally.

Every single instance,
A painful, bitter trance.

Notes to self

Let me vent out all my resentment against the narc in as many pages as I need to. (Burn the pages after that as a gesture releasing the resentment.)

How I deal with the resentment

The resentment I was carrying was killing me inside. There was a time when my whole body would ache with anger exploding out of every pore. I feared I would fall sick if I carried the anger within me any longer.

I prayed earnestly, asking God to give me the strength to forgive him. It felt impossible. The anger was overwhelming. While I was on a spiritual journey, the weight magically and palpably lifted off my heart. When I returned home, I no longer felt anger looking at him. I did not feel any emotion. Tears stopped welling up. I was finally at peace.

To prevent a buildup of resentment because of everyday exposure to the narc, I practice gratitude, do free-form journaling, and pray daily.

Notes to self

How far or close am I to forgiving the narc? What am I willing to do to heal myself so that I can forgive him and, in turn, be healed?

“We should be choosing what we want to keep and not what we want to get rid of.”

Marie Kondo

Forgotten abuse

Forgotten abuse

Sixth month of pregnancy
a quiet Saturday afternoon
Jigsaw pieces on floor
Left halfway done
TBD tomorrow
Don't touch them, you said
Help sweeping next morning
Shifted it unheard
Ruckus followed
Till dusk
Sorries scorned
Tired and big-bellied
Weeping and apologizing
Startled, as I felt
Spit on the face
Petrified!
This is what you deserve
He sniggered

Notes to self

What are some of the unacceptable instances of abuse, if any, that I have endured?

What I wish I had done about past abuse

I wish I had acted and given firm consequences when the abuse had happened.

It was reason enough to walk out, compounded by the gaslighting, manipulation, and emotional abuse that I had already been enduring.

However, I was a fearful person then with no confidence to survive on my own, being pregnant at that time. So, I lived on.

When I look back, some of these abuses happened sixteen years ago. Now they hold no relevance in the eyes of law. The reason they did not recur is because I became rebellious over time. He lost control over me. But at the same time, I lost an important legal argument.

Notes to self

Have I lived on with the narc after a significant incident? If yes, what made me do so? How do I wish I had reacted?

“Relationships with narcissists are held in place by hope of a ‘someday better’ with little hope or evidence to support it will ever arrive.”

Melanie Tonia Evans

Patriarchy

Patriarchy

Cosmo girl
Loved her large family of in-laws
A breath of fresh air from being nuclear
Dearly adored them
Especially his sisters
Still do

Our ways poles apart
They, religious and super-conservative
I, a dreamy girl with
a modern outlook
I accepted and
adjusted

One glaring instance that shook me, literally
MIL, his duplicate or he, her's
Visiting parents treated like servants, or
worse
Working, educated, dignified people
reduced to being servile
They endured for daughter's postpartum care
As their love outweighed

Outraged by their humiliation
I objected to his silence
Furious, red-faced
He held me by the throat
Flung me to the floor
C-section still fresh

He had made it clear
Questioning his mom
Was out of the question
The roots of patriarchy
Laid bare.

Why I am calling out the patriarchy

I believe the narcissism in men has its roots deep in the patriarchal ways of society.

When boys are raised with entitlement and made to believe that they are the superior gender, they turn out to be egotistical.

In patriarchal societies, men are the power centre and control how women are supposed to live. Men, therefore, lack empathy and put their needs front and centre. They don't think they are being unfair and normalize emotional and physical abuse.

Notes to self

Have I suffered because of any societal stereotypes? How do I explain it?

“Your pain didn’t start with you but it can end with you.”

Mark Wolynn

My turn

My turn

Blinded by love,
Played a rigged game all along.
A silly heart,
Abided by the rules.
A benchwarmer, with no choice,
A naive fool,
A puppet on a string.

Now, the tables have turned,
A new game has begun.
Every roll, a six,
A perfect, vengeful fix.
Let's play,
A game of retribution.

Squirming and writhing,
He pleads a last chance.
Love-bombing,
Lambasting,
Lamenting betrayal,
Sneaking a wayward glance,
Eyeing for a thaw.
His camouflage in splinters.

My fearless honest moves,
Deem him powerless.

Sitting on pins and needles,
All he gets to see,
An unstirred soul,
Piercing his veil,
Beyond manipulation.

What's my endgame

My end game is to end the relationship, simple. The narc and I don't belong in the same physical, emotional, or spiritual space.

My end game is to live a wholesome life, the best revenge against a narc. I want to grow in every facet of life, putting the past behind me. I want to be so fabulous that the narc cannot stand in the light of my truth and brilliance.

Fearless and blissful—that's my end game.

Notes to self

What will my end game look like?

“Still, I rise.”

Maya Angelou

Suggested resources

Video resources

1. Narc abuse recovery channels on YouTube: Melanie Tonia Evans, DoctorRamani, Prof. Sam Vaknin, Danish Bashir

2. Sadhguru's talks, YouTube

3. Naval Ravikant's talks and interviews, YouTube

4. Bad Sisters (Apple TV) to understand a narc's sabotaging personality

5. Abraham Hicks Publications, YouTube

Books

1. Untamed by Glennon Doyle

2. Daring Greatly by Brene Brown

3. The Power of Now by Eckhart Tolle

4. Can't Break Me by David Goggins

5. Never Split the Difference by Chris Voss

6. Atomic Habits by James Clear
7. Grit by Angela Duckworth
8. It Didn't Start With You by Mark Wolynn
9. The Courage To Be Disliked by Ichiro Kishim and Fumitake Koga
10. Meditations by Marcus Aurelius
11. The Subtle Art Of Not Giving A F*Ck by Mark Manson
12. The Life-Changing Magic of Tidying Up by Marie Kondo
13. Thinking Fast And Slow by Daniel Kahneman

9 789367 397053

Printed by Libri Plureos GmbH in Hamburg, Germany